This book is presented to:

_____

Date:

_____

On the special occasion of:

_____

I want to be Just like Jesus

BIBLE STORYBOOK

CREATED BY
Stephen Elkins

TYNDALE
K!DS

Tyndale House Publishers, Inc.
Carol Stream, Illinois

Visit Tyndale's website for kids at www.tyndale.com/kids.

TYNDALE is a registered trademark of Tyndale House Publishers, Inc. The Tyndale Kids logo is a trademark of Tyndale House Publishers, Inc. *Wonder Kids* is a trademark of The Stephens Group, Inc., DBA Wonder Workshop. *That End with a Hug!, Share-a-Hug!,* the Share-a-Hug! logo, and *Share a Hug with Someone You Love* are trademarks of Wonder Kids.

Just Like Jesus Bible Storybook

Created by Stephen Elkins

Cover illustration copyright © Ruth Zeglin. All rights reserved.

Cover border by Ed J Brown/Creative Market. All rights reserved.

Vector illustrations by Olga Zakharova/Creative Market. All rights reserved.

Interior illustrations by Simon Taylor-Kielty and Ruth Zeglin, copyright © by Stephen Elkins. All rights reserved. Interior illustrations by Mark Jones, copyright © by Tyndale House Publishers, Inc. All rights reserved.

All Scripture quotations, unless otherwise indicated, are taken from the *Holy Bible*, New Living Translation, copyright © 1996, 2004, 2007, 2013 by Tyndale House Foundation. Used by permission of Tyndale House Publishers, Inc., Carol Stream, Illinois 60188. All rights reserved.

Scripture quotations marked NIV are taken from the Holy Bible, *New International Version,*® NIV.® Copyright © 1973, 1978, 1984, 2011 by Biblica, Inc.® Used by permission. All rights reserved worldwide.

For manufacturing information regarding this product, please call 1-800-323-9400.

Library of Congress Cataloging-in-Publication Data

Elkins, Stephen, author.
  Just like Jesus Bible storybook / created by Stephen Elkins.
      pages cm. -- (Wonder kids)
   Audience: Ages 4-7.
   Audience: K to grade 3.
   ISBN 978-1-4964-0821-1 (hc)
1. Jesus Christ--Example--Juvenile literature. 2. Jesus Christ--Teachings--Juvenile literature.
3. Children--Religious life--Juvenile literature. I. Title.
  BT304.2.E44 2015
  248.8'2--dc23   2015014980

Printed in China

21   20   19   18   17   16
 7   6   5   4   3   2

Table of Contents

Those who say they live in God should live their lives as Jesus did.

1 JOHN 2:6

Dear Parents and Grandparents,

The ability to make good choices begins with good CHARACTER. In this book, we have identified 40 character traits Jesus demonstrated that can be taught to your child or grandchild.

There is no better place to begin a character study than with the life of Jesus. When applied to everyday living, we can walk as Jesus walked ... live as Jesus lived! What are some examples of these character traits? Jesus was generous, helpful, good, humble, hardworking, joyful, kind, obedient, patient, persistent, respectful, responsible, and truthful ... to mention only a few.

Each story in this book begins with JESUS IN THE BIBLE. This section highlights a particular character trait of Jesus. It tells a classic Bible story in a FUN-FILLED way that demonstrates the character of Jesus. It is followed by the JESUS IN ME section, which applies that character trait to everyday living—because we want to be *JUST LIKE JESUS!*

Building good character in children is progressive. So we close each story with a prayer asking God to help the children in our lives grow a greater love for others ... greater patience or kindness ... a greater degree of the featured character trait. Your child will love the conversational style of the stories. They are EASY TO READ and UNDERSTAND. Start your child on a journey toward a LIFETIME of character that is ... JUST LIKE JESUS!

Stephen Elkins

Jesus was Dependent

The Son can do nothing by himself. He does only what he sees the Father doing. Whatever the Father does, the Son also does.

JOHN 5:19

Everyone loves a superhero! Jesus was the greatest superhero of all. He sprang into action to heal sick people, calm storms, and walk on water!

But He didn't perform exciting miracles all by Himself.
He only did what He saw His Father in heaven doing! Jesus showed us the right way to live. We must depend on God's wisdom and power!

Have you ever ridden in an airplane? You probably couldn't see the pilot flying the plane. But you could still hear the pilot's voice. In the same way, you can't see God. But you can DEPEND on Him to guide you. His Word is true!

Prayer for Today

Lord, I want to be Your little superhero! Help me to depend on YOUR wisdom and power, not on my own strength.

To be just like Jesus...

I WILL BE DEPENDENT ON GOD.

13

Jesus was Thankful

Taking the five loaves and the two fish and looking up to heaven, [Jesus] gave thanks and broke the loaves. Then he gave them to his disciples to distribute to the people.

MARK 6:41, NIV

14

Talk about "fast food!" A hungry crowd of 5,000 people waited to eat. But Jesus had only five loaves of bread and two fish!

Jesus took the food, lifted it up to heaven, and thanked His heavenly Father. Then a miracle happened! That LITTLE bit of food became A LOT ... and fast! Everyone ate all they wanted!

Your mom and dad have taught you to say thank you when people do nice things for you. Saying thank you shows that you appreciate what they have done. That's why you should thank God every day for all the good things He has done!

Prayer for Today

Lord, teach me to be THANKFUL for all that You have done for me.

To be just like Jesus...

I WILL BE THANKFUL.

Jesus was Responsible

If you are faithful in little things, you will be faithful in large ones.

LUKE 16:10

JESUS IN THE BIBLE

"Responsible" is a big word! It means you do what you've been asked. Jesus told us that little jobs, if done well, will lead to more important ones.

God gave Jesus a BIG job to do. He taught us about God and forgave our sins on the cross. Jesus did everything His heavenly Father asked. That's being responsible!

Being RESPONSIBLE means that you do what you've been asked. When the job is done, you're ready to show others your good work. And just like Jesus, you'll hear God say, "Well done!"

Prayer for Today

Lord, help me to be responsible and do what You ask. I want my life to please You!

To be just like Jesus...

I WILL BE RESPONSIBLE.

Jesus was Spirit-Filled

After his baptism . . . [Jesus] saw the Spirit of God
descending like a dove and settling on him.

MATTHEW 3:16

22

Jesus was perfect. So why did He come to be baptized? He had no sin to wash away! When Jesus came up out of the water, God's Holy Spirit filled His heart.

It was time to start His mission! Jesus came to teach us about God and to forgive our sins. The Holy Spirit gave Jesus the power to do it!

When we ask Jesus to forgive our sins, we give God control of our lives. Then He fills us with His Holy Spirit. When we are full of God's Holy Spirit, His love controls our actions. Now we can be just like Jesus!

Prayer for Today

Lord, I want to be
SPIRIT-FILLED!
I pray for more and
more of Your Holy
Spirit each day.

To be just like Jesus...

I WILL BE SPIRIT-FILLED.

25

Jesus was Selfless

[Jesus] said to the crowd, "If any of you wants to be my follower, you must turn from your selfish ways, take up your cross daily, and follow me."

LUKE 9:23

26

JESUS IN THE BIBLE

Jesus told us what we must do to follow Him. First, stop being selfish. Be SELFLESS instead! Think about others' needs before your own.

Second, give up whatever stops you from serving Jesus. Then, let Jesus be your leader. The world around us says, "Do what YOU want to do." But Jesus says, "Do what GOD wants you to do!"

If we want to follow Jesus, we must change our direction. Let's stop being selfish and start serving Jesus. That's the pathway to heaven!

Prayer for Today

Lord, I want to be SELFLESS, just like You. Help me to follow You—every day, in every way!

To be just like Jesus...

I WILL BE SELFLESS.

29

Jesus was Caring

[Jesus said,] "I am the good shepherd. . . .
So I sacrifice my life for the sheep."

JOHN 10:14-15

Stop! That's what Jesus did when He saw someone in need. He cared too much to just pass by! He wanted to help. Jesus was like a caring shepherd who took care of His sheep.

Even today, Jesus takes good care of us. We are His sheep! Jesus showed us that "caring" is an action word. He is the Good Shepherd!

Jesus showed us how to be caring—like a shepherd cares for his sheep. And Jesus gave us a wonderful reason for caring. He said that caring for others is just like caring for Him. So when you share your lunch or visit a sick friend, it's as if you're doing it for Jesus Himself! Wow!

Prayer for Today

Lord, help me to be just like You and take time to CARE for others. Thank You for being my Good Shepherd!

To be just like Jesus...

I WILL BE CARING.

Jesus was Humble

[Jesus] humbled himself in obedience to God.

PHILIPPIANS 2:8

Even though Jesus was the King of kings, He humbled Himself and became a servant. He served God, and He served people. Why? Because He chose to obey His Father, God.

God asked Jesus to die on a cross so we could be saved. Jesus didn't have to! But He wanted to please God more than Himself. That's being humble!

JESUS IN ME

What does it mean to HUMBLE ourselves? It means that we choose to do things God's way. Doing things OUR way sounds good. But God's way is always better. So let's choose to serve and obey the King of kings! This might be a hard lesson, but it's worth it!

Prayer for Today

Lord, help me to be Your humble servant. Help me do things YOUR way. I want to please you!

To be just like Jesus...

I WILL BE HUMBLE.

Jesus showed Love

Just as I have loved you, you should love each other.

JOHN 13:34-35

Jesus didn't JUST say we should love each other. He said we should love each other the same way He loved us! How did Jesus show us His love?

By dying on the cross to forgive our sins. Jesus showed us that love isn't just a warm and fuzzy feeling. It's choosing to put someone else's need before our own!

"Jesus loves me—this I know!" Say that again. Except this time, shout out "ME" and point to your chest. Ready? "Jesus loves ME—this I know!" That was fun. And it's true! Do you want to be just like Jesus? Choose to show LOVE to others!

Prayer for Today

Lord, show me how
to love others—
even those who
are unkind to me.

To be just like Jesus...

I WILL SHOW LOVE.

Jesus was Dependable

Jesus Christ is the same yesterday, today, and forever.

HEBREWS 13:8

JESUS IN THE BIBLE

Perfect? Yes, Jesus is perfect! That's why Jesus is perfectly dependable! He always did exactly what He promised. Jesus told His helpers He would die on a cross.

But He promised that He would come back to life. Could they depend on Jesus? Yes! Three days later, His helpers visited His grave. It was EMPTY! Jesus was alive!

JESUS IN ME

To be like Jesus, learn to be DEPENDABLE! If you say you'll be somewhere at eight o'clock, be on time! If you promise to feed your dog, do it every day. Dependable people always do what they say they will do—just like Jesus!

Prayer for Today

Lord, help me to be a person others can depend on. Help me to do what I say I will do!

To be just like Jesus...

I WILL BE DEPENDABLE.

45

Jesus was Persistent

Keep on asking, and you will receive what you ask for. Keep on seeking, and you will find. Keep on knocking, and the door will be opened to you.

LUKE 11:9

JESUS IN THE BIBLE

Never give up on God! That's the lesson Jesus taught. He said,

"Don't just ask God for something once. Be persistent! Don't stop praying until you have God's answer. Keep seeking God's Word. It's like if you keep knocking on a door—soon enough, someone will come to open it. So keep knocking until that big door is opened!"

How many times must we pray
before our prayers are answered?
Once? Twice? Three times? More?
Be PERSISTENT! Never give
up until the answer comes!

Prayer for Today

Lord, when I am tempted to give up, help me pray one more time. Thank You for promising to answer me!

To be just like Jesus...

I WILL BE PERSISTENT.

Jesus was Sincere

Let us go right into the presence of God with sincere hearts.

HEBREWS 10:22

Jesus said that when we pray, we should be "sincere." Sincere people speak and act honestly. No faking it! They pray because they love God.

Some people pray so that others can see them and think they are nice. But God looks at our hearts. He knows why we are praying. That's why Jesus taught us to pray with sincere hearts!

When we are SINCERE, we are truthful about our feelings. When you speak, only say things you really mean. Don't ask someone "How are you?" unless you really want to know. Don't do something nice because others are watching you—do it because you sincerely care! And when you pray, talk to God from your heart.

Prayer for Today

Lord, help me have a sincere heart when I pray. May I do good things for Your glory and not my own!

To be just like Jesus...

I WILL BE SINCERE.

Jesus had Hope

Our hope is in the living God.

1 TIMOTHY 4:10

JESUS IN THE BIBLE

Jesus knew what would happen. People would treat Him badly, and He would die on a cross. Jesus was sad, but He didn't give up. Why?

He had hope! Hope isn't a wish. Hope is believing that God will always do what He says. And God promised to raise Jesus from the grave! Jesus had hope because He believed God!

Just like Jesus, we have HOPE! Hope isn't a wish that MIGHT come true. We find hope when we believe the promises of God. He promised to love us and watch over us. So no matter what happens, don't lose hope! God will always do what He promises ... for sure!

Prayer for Today

Lord, You are my hope. You will bless me because I believe Your promises!

To be just like Jesus...

I WILL HAVE HOPE.

Jesus was Patient

If you suffer for doing good and endure it
patiently, God is pleased with you.

1 PETER 2:20

JESUS IN THE BIBLE

You must be very patient to catch a fish! Jesus showed us how to be patient. He spent three whole years teaching people about God's love.

He was never in a hurry. He even prayed for people who did unkind things. He knew they were lost and needed His love. Jesus was "fishing" for people who would love Him back!

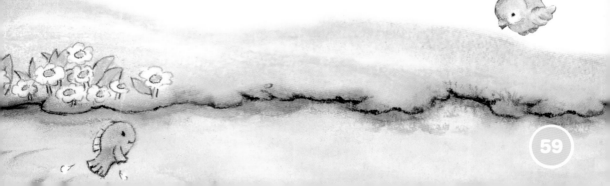

Having "patience" is trusting God enough to wait. It's like this: If someone is unkind to you, don't say something mean to that person. Wait for God to give you kind words instead. God is pleased when we show patience!

Prayer for Today

Lord, if unkind things are said to me, help me to be PATIENT. Thank You that I serve Jesus! He, too, showed patience in this world.

To be just like Jesus...

I WILL BE PATIENT.

Jesus was
Content

I have learned to be content with whatever I have.

PHILIPPIANS 4:11

Good is good! We can always find something to thank Him for. That's the secret of real contentment! Jesus was content, no matter what.

He didn't have a lot of money or things. He didn't even have a home. But He was happy anyway. Jesus never focused on what He didn't have. Instead, He thanked God for what He DID have.

Jesus never wanted more than God had given. To be like Jesus, we must believe that God knows best. We should think about all the good things God has given us—not about what we don't have. When we are thankful, we learn to be CONTENT!

Prayer for Today

Lord, thank You that You know best. Help me think about all the good things You have given me. Then I will be content!

To be just like Jesus...

I WILL BE CONTENT.

Jesus was Faithful

Well done, my good and faithful servant.

MATTHEW 25:21

Faithfulness brings a blessing! The Bible tells us that Jesus was faithful. He never once broke a promise! Jesus once told a story about a faithful servant.

"Take care of my money until I return from my trip," his master told him. The servant did just that! When the master returned, he was happy. "Well done!" he said. "Let's celebrate!"

JESUS IN ME

Jesus was FAITHFUL! He followed God's plan, and God rewarded Him. Your faithfulness will be rewarded too! If you are faithful to do little jobs for Mom and Dad, even bigger things will come your way. Faithfulness always brings a blessing!

Prayer for Today

Lord, help me to be faithful in the little things. Then You will trust me with bigger things!

To be just like Jesus...

I WILL BE FAITHFUL.

69

Jesus was Merciful

Await the mercy of our Lord Jesus Christ,
who will bring you eternal life.

JUDE 1:21

JESUS IN THE BIBLE

Bible study with Jesus! Jesus taught, and the crowd listened. Suddenly the roof started falling! A man on a stretcher came down through the hole.

The man couldn't walk, but his friends knew Jesus could help. When Jesus saw him, He had mercy and healed him! "Stand up," Jesus said. The man jumped up! Mercy is helping those who cannot help themselves.

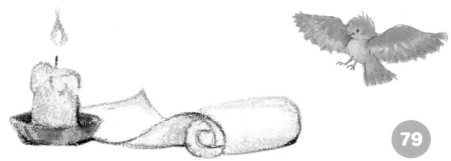

CRASH! Oh my. A bird flew into the window! The little fellow was lying still. We picked him up and gently placed him in a shoe box. Soon he got better and flew away. MERCY is helping those who cannot help themselves!

Prayer for Today

Lord, I want to be merciful to others. Show me how to help them whenever I can!

To be just like Jesus...

I WILL BE MERCIFUL.

Jesus showed Endurance

Because of the joy awaiting him, [Jesus] endured the cross.

HEBREWS 12:2

God made the first people, Adam and Eve, to live forever. But they disobeyed God, and then everything started to die. What could Adam do? Nothing!

But God could! He sent Jesus to endure the cross. To "endure" means to keep going, even when you'd like to quit. The cross was painful. But Jesus didn't quit until God's work was done!

Jesus gave His life to fix the problem of death. Now we can live forever, just the way God planned it! But first we must come to Jesus and ask Him to forgive our sins. Then we keep trusting Him through good times and bad. We endure and grow strong, just like Jesus did! His love keeps us going!

Prayer for Today

Lord, when things get hard, help me not to quit. Help me to show ENDURANCE, just like You!

To be just like Jesus...

I WILL SHOW ENDURANCE.

Jesus had Compassion

Moved with compassion, Jesus reached out and touched
him. "I am willing," he said. "Be healed!"

MARK 1:41

JESUS IN THE BIBLE

What size is your heart? It takes a big heart to show us what this big word means: "compassion." Jesus showed compassion to a man who was sick with leprosy.

"Help me!" the man begged. Jesus stopped what He was doing, reached out, and healed him! Jesus didn't want the man to be sick. His big heart was full of compassion!

Zoooom! The lightning flashed, and the rain poured down. Daddy stopped the car. A little puppy sat shivering by the roadside! We greeted the pup with a towel and lots of hugs. Bighearted COMPASSION reaches out to help those in need—even cute little puppies!

Prayer for Today

Lord, help me to show compassion by stopping and listening to people who need help.

To be just like Jesus...

I WILL HAVE COMPASSION.

Jesus worked Hard

Jesus replied, "My Father is always working, and so am I."

JOHN 5:17

JESUS IN THE BIBLE

Jesus was always at work, even as a boy! One day, Jesus' parents couldn't find Him. They searched everywhere. Where was He? At work in the church!

Jesus had a job to do.
His workplace was planet Earth.
He traveled to many places
and taught people about God's
Kingdom. Jesus worked very hard
to show us God's saving love!

JESUS IN ME

One day you, too, will have a job. You'll work to earn the money you'll need to live. But did you know there's another kind of work? Studying God's Word, singing in the church choir, telling your friends about Jesus—that's working for the Lord!

Prayer for Today

Lord, I don't want to be lazy. Help me to WORK HARD for You!

To be just like Jesus...

I WILL WORK HARD.

Jesus was Generous

Give, and you will receive. Your gift will return to you in full—pressed down, shaken together to make room for more, running over, and poured into your lap.

LUKE 6:38

What does it mean to be "generous"? Jesus watched people give their offerings at church. Many rich people gave lots of money. But they could have given more!

Then a woman gave only two coins. But she wasn't rich like the others. Jesus told His helpers, "This woman gave MORE than the rich people. She gave all the money she had!"

What does God care about the most? Is it the amount of money we give? Or is it the amount of love we give Him? Jesus wants us to be GENEROUS for the right reasons. Give because you love Him!

Prayer for Today

Lord, thank You that Jesus gave His life for me. Help me to give generously, just like Jesus!

To be just like Jesus...

I WILL BE GENEROUS.

Jesus was Devoted

No one can serve two masters. For ... you will be
devoted to one and despise the other. You
cannot serve both God and money.

LUKE 16:13

JESUS IN THE BIBLE

Time to decide! Jesus told us there are two masters. But we can only be devoted to ONE. The first is God. He is the Good Master who wants our complete devotion.

That means we give Him our time, money, and talents. The second is money. Money buys things. But it cannot buy God. Jesus made HIS choice. He served God!

What are you devoted to? You use your time seeking it, your talent sharing it, and your treasure serving it. God wants us to be devoted to HIS service. That's what devotion is—giving our all for God!

Prayer for Today

Lord, help me to seek
You with all my heart.
I want to be DEVOTED
to You alone!

To be just like Jesus...

I WILL BE DEVOTED
TO GOD.

Jesus was Encouraging

Don't let your hearts be troubled. Trust in God, and trust also in me.

JOHN 14:1

It couldn't be true! While eating supper with His helpers, Jesus told them He was going away. Peter wanted to go with Jesus. He was sad when Jesus said, "Not yet."

But then Jesus encouraged them all. "Don't be troubled," He said. "I'm going away to prepare a place for you. When everything is ready, I'll come back to get you!"

Sometimes life can be discouraging. Maybe your friend kicked the soccer ball the wrong way, and the game was lost. It's true—it was a big mistake. But that's when you need to use ENCOURAGING words! Say, "You'll do better next time!"

Prayer for Today

Lord, help me to build others up with encouraging words!

To be just like Jesus...

I WILL BE ENCOURAGING.

Jesus was Sensitive

"If I can just touch his robe, I will be healed." Immediately ... she could feel in her body that she had been healed of her terrible condition.

MARK 5:28-29

This poor woman had been sick for twelve long years! Not one doctor could help her. "I'm going to see Jesus!" she said. There was a big crowd around Him.

She came up behind Jesus and touched His clothes. "Who touched Me?" Jesus asked. He didn't see her! But He knew she had been healed. He was sensitive to her need!

JESUS IN ME

When they see a need, sensitive people are ready to help others. Like when your friend has a sad look on her face. Or when someone in your family is crying. Giving a hug says, "I love you. Can I help?" Don't wait for someone to ask you for help . . . be SENSITIVE, just like Jesus!

Prayer
for Today

Lord, help me to
be sensitive to the
needs of others.

To be just like Jesus...

I WILL BE SENSITIVE.

Jesus was Obedient

[Jesus] returned to Nazareth . . . and was obedient to them.

LUKE 2:51

JESUS IN THE BIBLE

When Jesus was a boy, He went with His parents to Jerusalem for a big celebration called Passover. Afterward, Mary and Joseph started home.

But they couldn't find Jesus! So they ran back to the city. They found Jesus at church, learning about God! When they returned home, Jesus obeyed His parents. By obeying His parents, Jesus was obeying God!

If you live on a busy street, your parents may have this rule: Stay out of the street! That rule keeps you safe. It says "I love you!" God's rules are like that too. His rules say "I love you!" When we are OBEDIENT to God and our parents, we are saying, "I love YOU, too!"

Prayer for Today

Lord, when I am tempted to disobey, help me remember that obeying the rules keeps me safe!

To be just like Jesus...

I WILL BE OBEDIENT.

Jesus had Peace

I am leaving you with a gift—peace of mind and heart.
And the peace I give is a gift the world cannot
give. So don't be troubled or afraid.

JOHN 14:27

JESUS IN THE BIBLE

Jesus is called the "Prince of Peace." Peace isn't the absence of troubles. Peace is the presence of Jesus! When Jesus is the Lord of our lives, our sins are forgiven.

Then we have peace with God. Only Jesus can give us that! With Jesus, we can "sleep in heavenly peace"—even when there are troubles in the world around us.

"God blesses those who work for peace," Jesus said. But to have PEACE, you must have Jesus in your life. Peace can't be found in the world around us. It's only found in Jesus. He calms our hearts and lets us sleep in heavenly peace!

Prayer for Today

Lord, thank You for forgiving my sins and giving me true peace!

To be just like Jesus...

I WILL HAVE PEACE.

Jesus was
Good

Let your good deeds shine out for all to see, so that
everyone will praise your heavenly Father.

MATTHEW 5:16

JESUS IN THE BIBLE

Jesus told us it's important to be good. Why? So that everyone can know about God's love and praise Him! Jesus always did the right thing. He was s-o-o-o-o-o good!

Jesus was good to the weak, good to the strong! He was good to the rich, good to the poor. His good deeds shone like lights in a dark room!

Good things are "God" things, like sharing and caring! Good kids are kind. They tell the truth, keep a promise, and do the things Jesus would do! If you're a good kid, you'll make new friends. Then you can tell them about God's love!

Prayer for Today

Lord, teach me how
to let my light shine.
I want to do the right
thing, at the right time,
for the right reason.
I want to be GOOD!

To be just like Jesus...

I WILL BE GOOD.

Jesus was Joyful

Jesus was filled with the joy of the Holy Spirit.

LUKE 10:21

Joy! It's a blessing that comes from God. Jesus was filled with heavenly joy. He never let anyone—or anything—take this special gift away. Not even knowing He would die on the cross!

Jesus never confused "joy" with "happiness." Happiness depends on things AROUND you. Joy depends on things INSIDE you! Obeying God was Jesus' greatest joy!

JESUS IN ME

There will be times when you are unhappy. Just remember—happiness depends on what is happening around you. But joy comes from God. So no matter what, let the joy of the Lord be your strength!

Prayer for Today

Lord, I know that joy is a gift from You. Help me to be JOYFUL, even when bad things happen!

To be just like Jesus...

I WILL BE JOYFUL.

Jesus was Meek

"Put away your sword," Jesus told him.

MATTHEW 26:52

Jesus was strong! He had God's great power. When Jesus went to the cross, He showed "meekness." Meekness is not weakness. It's having power but using it wisely.

Jesus could have asked God to send angels to rescue Him! Instead, He chose to die. He showed meekness and won a great victory on that cross. He forgave our sins!

JESUS IN ME

Only two people in the Bible are called "MEEK": Moses and Jesus. Both were strong and mighty men! But they still listened to God. Even if obeying Him was hard sometimes. Meekness isn't weakness. It is strength under control!

Prayer for Today

Lord, if I am faster or better at something than my friends are, help me to show meekness. May I slow down and help them!

To be just like Jesus...

I WILL BE MEEK.

Jesus was Helpful

The LORD is my helper.

HEBREWS 13:6

Thirty-eight years! That's how long one man had been sick. He was lying down by a pool of water when Jesus came along. Jesus asked, "Do you want to get well?"

"I can't," the man said. "I have no one to help me!" Then Jesus helped the man like no one else could. He healed him! The man walked away glad!

Being HELPFUL was a way of life for Jesus. And He wants us to be good helpers too. What can we do to help others? Be aware—always care and always share! When you see someone who needs help, be just like Jesus!

Prayer for Today

Lord, help me to be aware when others need help. May I always care and always share!

To be just like Jesus...

I WILL BE HELPFUL.

Jesus told the Truth

[Jesus said,] "I was born and came into the world to testify to the truth."

JOHN 18:37

JESUS IN THE BIBLE

Jesus had been arrested. A judge asked Him, "Are you a king?" Jesus answered, "I am the King of heaven! I came to tell people the truth."

"What is truth?" the judge asked. JESUS! His Word is the truth. Loving Him is the only way we get to heaven. Jesus gave His life on the cross for you and me!

JESUS IN ME

The Bible says that Jesus is the way, the TRUTH, and the life. We must always tell the truth. Jesus did, even when it cost Him His life! Truth doesn't depend on where we are or who we're talking to. To be like Jesus, we tell the truth, and we do it with a loving heart! What is truth? Jesus is truth!

Prayer for Today

Lord, help me to always tell the truth. Thank You that Jesus always did so. Thank You that He IS the truth!

Jesus was Gentle

Let the children come to me. Don't stop them! For the Kingdom of God belongs to those who are like these children.

MARK 10:14

Jesus was strong, like a lion! He drove the money changers out of God's church. But He was also gentle, like a lamb.

When His helpers wouldn't let moms and dads bring their kids to Him, Jesus was sad! "Let them come," He said. "Children need My love too!" Gentleness is a soft touch and a pleasant word.

Have you ever spent time with a baby? If so, an adult may have told you, "Be GENTLE with the baby!" Jesus was gentle with children. Being gentle doesn't mean you are weak. It means you choose to use a soft touch with those who are weaker than you are.

Prayer for Today

Lord, help me to be gentle with those who are weak.

To be just like Jesus...

I WILL BE GENTLE.

Jesus had a Pure Heart

God blesses those whose hearts are pure,
for they will see God.

MATTHEW 5:8

One day, on a mountainside, Jesus taught something important: People who have pure hearts find favor with God! Their hearts are sparkling clean because Jesus did the cleaning up!

He washed away their sins when He died on the cross. Those with pure hearts love God and want to live for Him alone. They are ready to see God!

For water to be clean and pure, it must not have anything bad in it. And if we are to be clean and pure before God, we must not have any sin in us. But how? When we ask Jesus to forgive us, He washes away our sins and makes us ready to see God! Are you ready?

Prayer for Today

Lord, You alone can forgive me and make my heart clean. Then I will have a PURE HEART, just like Jesus!

To be just like Jesus...

I WILL HAVE
A PURE HEART.

Jesus was Confident

Seek the Kingdom of God above all else, and live righteously, and he will give you everything you need.

MATTHEW 6:33

"No worries!" That's what you say when you're confident. Jesus showed us how to live with confidence by pointing to our feathered friends!

"Look at the birds," He said. "They don't worry about what they'll eat, because God feeds them!" So turn your cares into confidence. You can trust God to take care of YOU, too!

147

There are a lot of worried people. But nobody has ever seen a worried bird! That's because God takes care of them! Do you want to be CONFIDENT? Get to know God—tell Him about what makes you happy and what makes you sad. Then trust Him to help. Know God—no worries!

Prayer for Today

Lord, as I grow up, help me to trust You to take care of my needs. Then I will have real confidence!

To be just like Jesus…

I WILL BE CONFIDENT.

Jesus was Friendly

Now you are my friends, since I have told
you everything the Father told me.

JOHN 15:15

A friend indeed! Time and time again, Jesus was friendly to others. He spoke to strangers and reached out to people who were sick or needy.

Jesus even asked God to forgive the Roman soldiers when they treated Him unkindly. What a friend we have in Jesus! He's your very best friend on earth—and in heaven!

Jesus loves everyone. We should do the same. A friendly spirit just flows out of people who love God. Being FRIENDLY brings people closer to us so we can tell them about God's love!

Prayer
for Today

Lord, help me to be
a friendly person so
that I can tell others
about Your love.

To be just like Jesus...

I WILL BE FRIENDLY.

Jesus was Forgiving

[Peter] asked, "Lord, how often should I forgive someone who sins against me? Seven times?" "No, not seven times," Jesus replied, "but seventy times seven!"

MATTHEW 18:21-22

Peter came to Jesus and asked, "If a person keeps doing bad things, should I forgive him 7 times?" That seems fair, doesn't it? Jesus surprised Peter with His answer:

"More than that! Take the number 70. Now add it together 7 times!" Oh my—that's 490 times! Jesus was telling Peter that his forgiveness should have no limits.

JESUS IN ME

Jesus tells us that our forgiveness should have no limits! When it's hard to forgive someone for doing bad things, just remember—Jesus did what He taught others to do. He even gave His own life on the cross so that WE might be forgiven! No limits!

Prayer for Today

Lord, help me learn to be like You by loving and FORGIVING without limits.

To be just like Jesus...

I WILL BE FORGIVING.

Jesus was Respectful

She said to Jesus, "You are a Jew, and I am a Samaritan woman. Why are you asking me for a drink?"

JOHN 4:9

"Respect." What does it mean? One day, Jesus stopped for a drink of water. There He met a woman from Samaria. Jesus lived in Judah, not Samaria.

Most men from Judah wouldn't even SPEAK to a Samaritan woman! But Jesus was polite. He treated her with kindness and respect. "I am the Savior!" He said. She believed and told others about Jesus!

The world is filled with all kinds of people. The color of their skin may be different from yours. They may speak other languages. But Jesus taught us to be RESPECTFUL of everyone. Why? Because God created each person, and He loves them all! Shouldn't we love them too?

Prayer for Today

Lord, I know I should not like some people more than others just because of how they look. Help me to respect everyone I meet, just like Jesus did.

To be just like Jesus...

I WILL BE RESPECTFUL.

Jesus was Decisive

Jesus went up on a mountain to pray, and he prayed to God all night. At daybreak he called together all of his disciples and chose twelve of them to be apostles.

LUKE 6:12-13

Decisions. Jesus always made good ones! One day, up on a mountain, He chose 12 men to help Him spread the Good News about God's Kingdom. How did Jesus know which men to choose?

He prayed to His Father, God, in heaven! Jesus prayed before making decisions, big or small. He called on the One who always knows the right thing to do!

"Good call!" Sports umpires have to make decisions in a split second! That's called being DECISIVE. You have to make decisions every day too. Some are more important than others. God knows what's up ahead. Spending time with Him will help you make good decisions!

Prayer for Today

Lord, I want to be decisive. Help me to ask You for help with every decision.

To be just like Jesus...

I WILL BE DECISIVE.

Jesus was
Wise

[Jesus said,] "Anyone who listens to my teaching and follows it is wise, like a person who builds a house on solid rock."

MATTHEW 7:24

Jesus told this story: One person built a house on top of sand. Another built a house on top of solid rock. The sun came out, and all was well!

But then came the clouds. It rained and rained! The house built on sand washed away. Bye-bye! But the house built on solid rock stood firm. Hurray! Which person was wise?

The two houses were the same—except for one thing: the foundation! Which foundation was weak? The sand! Which was strong? The rock! If you pay attention to the lessons Jesus taught in the Bible, you are WISE. You are choosing to build your life on the right foundation—solid rock! Anything else is sinking sand!

Prayer
for Today

Lord, help me to be
wise and obey what
You taught us in the
Bible. I want to be
just like Jesus!

To be just like Jesus...

I WILL BE WISE.

☑ To be Just like Jesus, I will...

101 Color & Sing BIBLE STORIES

CREATED BY STEPHEN ELKINS

INCLUDES 2 DISCS

978-1-4143-9019-2

ECPA MEDALLION OF EXCELLENCE

Christian Book Award®

From *MULTIMILLION–SELLING author & songwriter Stephen Elkins*

Read it! Sing it!
Color it! Remember it!

- 101 easy-to-read Bible stories with colorful art
- 101 sing-along Bible songs on 2 CDs
- 101 fun facts about the Bible
- PLUS 101 printable coloring pages

CP0976

Children love getting hugs as
much as they love giving them!

Snuggle Time Devotions That End with a Hug! features 52
activity-based devotions that let children know they are loved
and cherished by God. And to make your time together an
extraspecial event, each story ends with a great big hug!

From
*MULTIMILLION–SELLING
author & songwriter
Stephen Elkins*

share a hug with someone you love.™

CP0977